Everyone is Equal

by Jayneen Sanders

illustrated by Cherie Zamazing

Using Little **BIG** Chats

The *Little BIG Chats* series has been written to assist parents, caregivers and educators to have open and age-appropriate conversations with young children around crucial, and yet at times, 'tough' topics. And what better way than using children's picture books! Some pages will have questions for your child to interact with and discuss. Feel free to use these questions and the Discussion Questions provided on the inside back cover of this book to help you assist your child with the topic being explored. Stop at any time to unpack the text together; and try to follow your child's lead wherever that conversation may take you! So, please, get comfy and start some empowering 'chats' around some BIG topics with your child.

The Body Safety titles should ideally be read in the following order: *Consent*, *My Safety Network*, *My Early Warning Signs*, *Private Parts are Private*, and *Secrets and Surprises*. The remaining titles can be read in any order.

Hi! I'm Belle.
Today we're learning
about all children
being exactly who
they are meant to be.

This is Theodore
and this is Jun.

Theodore and Jun are my friends. We go to the same kindergarten.

DO YOU HAVE A SPECIAL FRIEND AT KINDERGARTEN OR SCHOOL?

At kindergarten we play with the wooden blocks.

We make towers that go up, up, up.

They go way up high.

And sometimes they fall down!

We like to play with
the cars and the trucks
on the big table.

Theodore loves the red car
and I love the blue car.

But Jun likes the
pink car best of all!

At kindergarten we love
to play dress-ups.

Sometimes we
dress up as firefighters.

And sometimes we
dress up as princesses.

And sometimes we dress up as pirates sailing on the sea.

WHAT DO YOU LIKE TO DRESS UP AS?

I love my friends.

They are just like me
in so many ways.

HOW ARE YOUR FRIENDS THE SAME AS YOU?

Theodore, Jun and I are equal.

Equal is a very important word.

It means that no matter:

- who you are,

- what you look like,

- what you can or can't do,

- or where you come from...

EVERYONE should be
treated the same.

15

People are special
in their own way.

But everyone is equal.